Facts About the Coyote

By Lisa Strattin

© 2019 Lisa Strattin

FREE BOOK

FREE FOR ALL SUBSCRIBERS

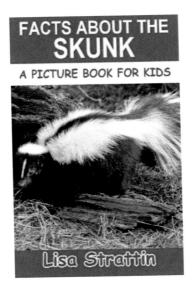

LisaStrattin.com/Subscribe-Here

BOX SET

- **FACTS ABOUT THE POISON DART FROGS**
- **FACTS ABOUT THE THREE TOED SLOTH**
  - **FACTS ABOUT THE RED PANDA**
  - **FACTS ABOUT THE SEAHORSE**
  - **FACTS ABOUT THE PLATYPUS**
  - **FACTS ABOUT THE REINDEER**
  - **FACTS ABOUT THE PANTHER**
- **FACTS ABOUT THE SIBERIAN HUSKY**

LisaStrattin.com/BookBundle

Facts for Kids Picture Books by Lisa Strattin

Little Blue Penguin, Vol 92

Chipmunk, Vol 5

Frilled Lizard, Vol 39

Blue and Gold Macaw, Vol 13

Poison Dart Frogs, Vol 50

Blue Tarantula, Vol 115

African Elephants, Vol 8

Amur Leopard, Vol 89

Sabre Tooth Tiger, Vol 167

Baboon, Vol 174

Sign Up for New Release Emails Here

LisaStrattin.com/subscribe-here

COVER IMAGE

ADDTIONAL IMAGES

Contents

INTRODUCTION

Coyotes, also known as the Prairie Wolf, are native to North and Central America. However, they are thought to have come from the European Grey Wolf. They are a separate species in their own right. They are different from wolves in vocal sound patterns, as well as how they live in their pack.

The coyote's scientific name, Canis latrans actually means barking dog.

CHARACTERISTICS

The coyote is able to reach sprinting speeds of around 40 miles per hour which they are able to maintain for extended periods of time. They can also jump to heights of up to 13 feet!

There are 19 different coyote subspecies with only 3 of these found in Central America. The remaining 16 subspecies can be found throughout Mexico, Canada and the USA.

Historically, the coyote has been nocturnal but now can often be seen during the day in areas where they are not threatened by humans. In areas where they are heavily hunted and trapped, they tend to still be nocturnal animals. They adapt very well to suburban life and can often be seen drinking out of swimming pools.

APPEARANCE

The coloring of the coyote varies considerably according to where they live. In the northernmost parts of their range, coyotes can be pale to almost white in color. In the west, they tend to be a rich reddish hue with black markings. In the plains states of the US, they are a plain greyish brown. The occasional black coyote is sometimes seen in the eastern states.

REPRODUCTION

The coyote mates between February and April. The female may mate with more than one male during a season. Two months after mating, the female gives birth to between one and nineteen pups! However, the average litter size is usually around six pups.

LIFE SPAN

Coyotes live for 10 to 15 years, on average, in the wild.

HABITAT

The coyote tends to stay in a burrow when not looking for food. They usually dig their own burrow, but will take over an empty badger burrow if it is possible. This den becomes the center of the coyote's territory which can extend to 11 miles around the den! The size of the territory depends on how much food is available nearby.

Coyotes tend to stay together in mated pairs, though in areas where large prey live alongside them, a loose pack structure has been noticed.

They are less social than wolves and their threat displays are much more primitive. They arch their backs and open their jaws, without the facial expressions that wolves have.

DIET

Coyotes prefer rabbit for dinner over all other choices. But they will eat deer and mice when they are available.

ENEMIES

Common predators that hunt coyotes include bears, cougars, wolves, mountain lions and even other coyotes. Dogs and eagles are also opportunistic predators against coyote pups.

SUITABILITY AS PETS

A coyote is a wild animal and not generally suitable to be a pet. You can probably see some at your local zoo if you want to watch them.

COLOR ME

COLOR ME

COLOR ME

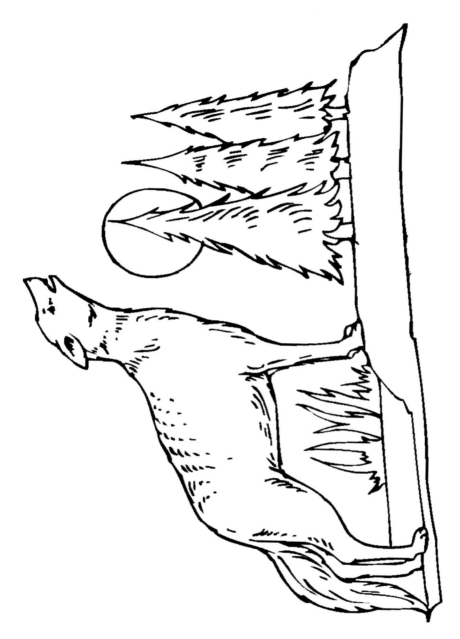

COLOR ME

COLOR ME

COLOR ME

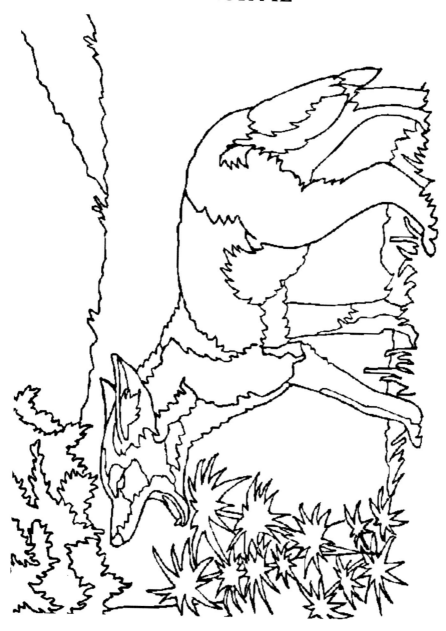

COLOR ME

Please leave me a review here:

LisaStrattin.com/Review-Vol-305

For more Kindle Downloads Visit Lisa Strattin Author Page on Amazon Author Central

amazon.com/author/lisastrattin

To see upcoming titles, visit my website at LisaStrattin.com– most books available on Kindle!

LisaStrattin.com

FREE BOOK

FOR ALL SUBSCRIBERS – SIGN UP NOW

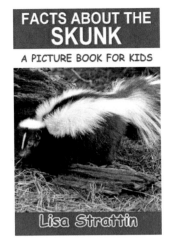

LisaStrattin.com/Subscribe-Here

LisaStrattin.com/Facebook

LisaStrattin.com/Youtube

Made in the USA
Las Vegas, NV
08 April 2024

88432262R00026